Preface

In reading this book, you will learn about some characters that you may encounter at work or in your personal life. These characters tend to have a detrimental impact on your ability to achieve things, and thus learning to effectively manage them will help you accomplish more.

From time to time, we all may act like some of the characters in this book. However, this book is not about occasional tendencies: This book is about those who frequently display similar traits as the characters.

Working with or managing people can be very complicated. In order to do this effectively, it is important to accept that each person is unique, making your capacity to use emotional intelligence very powerful. It is not always practical to cater for the complete spectrum of differences and some people do have shared, common characteristics. This book will not provide an exact classification system, but will identify common tendencies and patterns across large groups of people. These tendencies and patterns are problematic for others in their effort to achieve things.

Some of the characters may not resonate with you, but, I am confident that some will. You may find yourself thinking: 'That sounds a lot like someone at work'. Perhaps you may find yourself thinking that you are one or more of the characters? If the latter applies…you are a problem!

Sometimes innocent things, like a snowflake can have devastating consequences when in large quantities and unmanaged…

A few people with similar negative characteristics may go unrecognised or be diluted in a business. The significance of such traits when in large quantities must be respected and addressed.

Human Resources

Having resources are essential in any context and if used well can contribute significantly. In contrast, having no resources can have devastating effects. Resources have a value and consequently tend to be controlled by supply and demand.

People are a business resource (Human Resources) and an important one at that, especially in knowledge intense industries. People can be the essence and sole of a company and core to its success. Some business leaders consider their employees as more important than their customers.

Without appropriate Human Resources a business is unlikely to develop and grow. A lack of investment in Human Resources can cause regression. Human Resources can also be considered a risk to a company. They can be expensive to attract, develop and retain. It is therefore very important to lead and manage people effectively, in fact many companies spend a lot of time and attention developing people strategies.

Attracting people to a company may be one thing, but attracting the right people is another. In the ever changing competitive landscape and where the room for error is marginal, the search and fight to keep talent is getting harder.

The notion of talent is vague and sometimes difficult to define or explain, but I would urge any business leader to spend time planning and defining what talent means to them. Learning what talent isn't after hiring someone is reactive and expensive.

As well as talent, people need to have a good attitude and behaviours. This too may need to be defined. People's personality traits can underpin success or undermine it. Aligning key characteristics to a role, a line manager or team can pay dividends. Psychometric testing is one way of getting an objective overview of someone's character. There is much debate over the value of psychometric testing and it must not be used in isolation from other evaluation strategies. Many argue that psychometric testing contributes significantly to the recruitment process by offering a fair way of assessing a potential employee. I have found value in psychometric testing, not only to assess a candidate, but to help understand the cohesion of a team and help choose the most appropriate management style to get the best results.

A Cheesy Metaphor

Running a business, managing a department or leading a team is a lot like gardening… bear with me, it will get better, I promise. Once you have decided on what you want your garden to look like, you need to set about achieving your vision. You must work on cultivating the flowers, fruit or vegetables in your garden, feeding, watering and pruning them.

In most cases, weeds will grow in your garden, which will be obvious to an experienced gardener, but not so much for others; myself included. Some weeds are hidden out of sight and it is important to weed out these plants for the greater good of the garden. Weeds soak up goodness from the soil and can thus hinder the growth of other plants you want. This book is about identifying and treating the 'weeds' (characters in this book) and gardening your business or team.

It is important to acknowledge these characters, whom must be contained and weeded out. No longer shall these characters remain hidden in the shadows or blind-spots of businesses. They can be the cancer of success and, just as you would react to such alarming and stark realisations in other parts of your life, you should act now!

Contents

Acknowledgements	Page 7
The Concept	Page 8
The Clever Stuff	Page 11
Child-like characteristics	Page 12
Chapter 1: Messers	Page 13
Chapter 2: Blaggers	Page 18
Chapter 3: Flappers	Page 25
Chapter 4: Duckers and Divers	Page 31
Chapter 5: Reactors	Page 36
Chapter 6: Magpies	Page 41
Chapter 7: Victims	Page 46
Chapter 8: Non-believers	Page 51
Chapter 9: Know-it-alls	Page 58
Chapter 10: Astronomers	Page 63
Chapter 11: Box Tickers	Page 68
Chapter 12: Cyclops	Page 75
Chapter 13: Ostriches	Page 81
Summary	Page 86
How to handle the characters	Page 90
Bibliography	Page 99

Acknowledgements

I would like to express my sincere gratitude and thanks to my remarkable family, for all their support and sacrifices.

Love and thanks to my father whom I have dedicated this book; a real man, to whom I am in eternal debt. A soldier of life.

The Conception

I can recall my first job straight out of university, where I worked for a large construction company. On my very first day, I was introduced to a gentleman, who kindly helped me to settle in. He was very keen to give me the low-down on everyone and everything within the company, in his own, slightly biased way. I will never forget the bitter cynicism in his voice when he stated that "most of the people who work here are Blaggers".

The man continued to explain, informing me that he himself was in fact a 'Blagger': This meant that he knew very little about his role; but boldly and convincingly lied about the level of knowledge he had. He seemed strangely proud of this fact. I found this naively funny at the time and was seemingly in denial, thinking, surely this can't be true? I thought, I am now in the serious world of work, working with adults in a large, successful corporate organisation. He must be joking?

How wrong I was, as I witnessed him go on to 'blag' his way through many different situations, turning a web of lies and convincing colleagues that he knew what to do. He told me he has made a career out of 'blagging', and was paid very well for this too.

As time went by, I began to lose confidence in my colleagues and the company I worked for. Was it this man's good fortune and skill if his blagging was undiscovered or was it a reflection of the management team or system that his 'blagging' went unrecognised?

I quickly realised that the lies of this Blagger was having a profoundly negative effect on achieving goals, caused ineffective planning and increased risks. More concerning was that some 'blags' had compromised safety. Therefore, the fact that the Blagger had gone undetected was not and should not be his good fortune. Something had to be done and it was. I also learnt the value of having strong leadership and robust management systems to detect such a risk.

A domino effect may happen from a 'blag' with overwhelming consequences, especially when Blaggers may become managers of other Blaggers. As this cycle perpetuates a weird blag vortex of hot air can be created which can engulf a company.

Over time I began to recognise other Blaggers in my workplace. I became adept at it, recognising this underhand artistry in full effect. I was able to dodge them and their blags, meaning I got more done and avoided embarrassing situations. Tragically, some people did not realise they were Blaggers. I was never sure which was worse: Those who knew they knew nothing and would play the game, or those that knew nothing and did not realise it, despite the bravado? I also began to recognise other types of characters that I felt were a hindrance to the company and to myself.

As my 'talent' for spotting these groups of people became tailored, I had various methods of recognising them, confirming their existence and making efforts to avoid or manage them. I began to taste the bitterness of cynicism and became a self-professed judge, feeling it was my duty to 'out' these people and label others: This became a bad habit, and one I regret. Thankfully, I refined my understanding of the personality traits these people possessed and vowed that the model I created would be used ethically and with care.

On that note; please do not use the information in this book to unethically prejudice, isolate, victimise or bully colleagues. Simply acknowledge that some employees possess these trait, know that they can hinder performance and take strides to manage them in a legal and ethical manner. Be careful with the knowledge and power contained within the book: The message is simple, but implementation must be handled with caution!

After taking control of these thoughts, compiling a list of characters and reminiscing about some of the experiences I have had, this book was conceived.

"I suppose leadership at one time meant muscles; but today it means getting along with people" - **Indira Gandhi**.

Clever Stuff

Attribution is a concept within social psychology, and is the method by which the causes of behaviour and events are explained. Research into attribution psychology has been around for many years, and has been extended to include how people perceive each other and how they account for each other's behaviour. There are two types of attribution psychology; **'explanatory attribution'** and 'interpersonal attribution'.

Explanatory attribution refers to when people ascribe a reason for a particular event happening, in order to make sense of it. People employ **explanatory attribution** to prevent any embarrassment and disguise the true reason for something happening, especially if it was their fault.

Interpersonal attribution refers to when the causes of the events involve two or more people, and is commonly used when the motives for actions are called into question. People use **interpersonal attribution** to present themselves in the most positive light.

Attributing reasons as to why goals are not achieved is important: Without knowing why such things happen, it is harder to be able to learn and thus prevent such things from happening again. It is important to make sense of a problem, and this book goes some way in doing that by identifying problematic characters (explanatory attributors) and suggests ways to address them.

Child-like characteristics

As William Claude Dukenfield famously quoted: *"Never work with animals or children"*.

I think children are great and I am simply infatuated by my children. Children by their nature will display certain characteristics, some general characteristics are:

- Effort is more important than perfection
- They change activities often and quickly
- They are emotionally sensitive and are thus vulnerable
- Generally, they are carefree
- They actively seek out approval
- They dislike any change to their routine
- Love and routine provide a sense of security
- They may be easily discouraged
- They cannot think chronologically (no concept of time)

Many adults, parents especially, can relate to the list and, for the most part, find the characteristics endearing. But, what if we relate these characteristics to an adult? Do you consider them charming now? What if you are relying on someone with these characteristics to get important things done? These child-like characteristics are common in the characters in this book and frankly cause problems.

Chapter 1: Messers

Who Are They?

A Messer is someone who procrastinates and rarely get things done on time. They always have an excuse; some farfetched and flippant. Their ineptitude commonly defines this character, but an Messer's competence is not always in question; they can have more ugly traits, like a distinct inability (often unknowingly) to prioritise. They rarely think clearly when getting things done, especially when faced with adversity. Messers will let people down with empty promises. Sometimes, Messers can be very indecisive and are unable to command and control a situation. Their comprehension of planning and ability to do it is poor, holding deadlines in low regard. Messers tend to have very little integrity in the eyes of their colleagues.

There are lots of ways to develop competence, which unfortunately not enough to change an Messer. Their behaviours are habitual, having evolved over a long period of time.

It is not uncommon for an Messer to feel overworked and can become a bluster of action when pressured to do so, often with no traction or effectiveness. The term 'busy fool' is apt for an Messer.

Messers tend to be disorganised and shy away from challenging tasks, especially in terms of confronting difficult, perhaps personal, situations. They postpone hard tasks, completing easy to achieve tasks first, and share many similarities with the Ostrich character (see Chapter 13). Messers simply cannot be trusted; their words are cheap and are rarely followed up with effective action. A state of embarrassing confusion can be created by employing or working alongside an Messer.

Real Example:

I once had the fortune of working with a person who in my opinion was the most fascinating Messer I have ever met. To be fair, he was responsible for serving a very demanding client and didn't we know it. Every opportunity to shout about the pressure he was under, was taken.

He was often found hidden away, chatting and complaining about his workload. He had convinced himself and made a lot of effort to convince others that he was indispensable to the company.

The Messer went on holiday and cover was appointed in his absence. It was found that the so-called demanding client was not as demanding as we thought.

The colleague in question returned and had very little work to do: It was all in hand. It was not long, however, before he was presented with a challenge from the client. He had to ensure that a manufactured product was painted, inspected and delivered to the client by the end of the week. This was a tight timescale, but was possible, providing no problems arose. My colleague approached this challenge by complaining, moaning and stalling. He continued to spin his usual line to others, procrastinating and doing all he could to prevent addressing the challenge. He spent the usual amount of time drinking coffee with his pals and visiting suppliers unnecessarily.

Needless to say, this gentleman did not turn any of this into effective action: The product was not delivered to the painters, as he had not organised transport. Other employees ended up working harder and later, in order to accommodate his failings. He had also forgotten to book transport for the product's return journey back to the factory, for inspection and packaging. He had not informed anyone that inspection was needed and to what extent.

Rather, this colleague opted to pick up the parts himself and inspect them, claiming that he was a team player and making every effort to show others how great he was. He fumbled, messed about, hid things, stalled and, in the end, missed the deadline. He then proceeded to blame all of the other departments, such as the transport and inspection departments for not supporting him, stating that he felt like he was running the company on his own. A true Messer.

The Clever Bit:

A common misperception is that people who procrastinate are lazy. This is not the case; in fact, it is often the opposite. Those that procrastinate waste valuable time, tending to work more intensely just before a deadline, and this is not laziness. Procrastinators often claim they work best under pressure, yet this stand-point must be challenged. They tend to make this claim when they are not working to a deadline, or they have forgotten the negative consequences of procrastinating. It is widely thought that they do so due to habit and routinely work without a plan, perhaps implementing one just before a deadline. Messers never approach tasks systematically, and this dramatically increases the risk of something going wrong.

This act is often a self-protection strategy; for example, if someone procrastinates, they always have the excuse of 'not having enough time', in the event that they fail, so that their sense of ability is never threatened.

There is a lot of pressure within the workplace: Pressure to meet deadlines and achieve targets. For the most part, the reasons for delaying and avoiding tasks are rooted in fear and anxiety of performing poorly, losing control of outcomes or looking stupid, and having one's sense of self or self-concept challenged. Messers avoid doing work, in order to avoid their abilities being judged. If they happen to succeed, they feel that much 'smarter'.

A Few Ways to Spot a Messer:

- They have no structure to their approach to things.
- They are weak at prioritising.
- They are poor at keeping promises or appointments.
- They procrastinate.
- They are indecisive.

What Impact Can They Have?

A Messer will waste time, miss deadlines, cause inefficiencies, raise hopes, over-promise and under deliver. They are costly to any organisation and costly to relationships. Their ineffectiveness is contagious and will result in standards slipping, with concessions made to accommodate them or help them meet deadlines. Fight the urge to do this: Messers hamper the possibility of targets being achieved and thus reduce prospects. If tolerated, this will cause an imbalance in expectations between groups of people within the workforce. The return on any investment in an Messer will be lower than that of other employees. There are high costs, in terms of lost opportunity, which may cause excessive pressure, frustration and stress amongst the workforce. An unhealthy amount of tension within teams and the larger workforce is counterproductive.

Philosophical Conclusion:

An insincere colleague is more to be feared than a wild beast - *Buddha.*

Chapter 2: Blaggers

Who Are They?

A Blagger is simply a bender of the truth at best. Blaggers are not trustworthy, and often say one thing and do something else. This can be frustrating, which will be amplified if people feel deceived or manipulated in some way.

When I left University, I was excited to begin my career and keen to work with professionals that I could shadow and learn from. When I started my first job, I quickly learnt that my expectations were naïve, especially in thinking that professionalism would be publicly displayed and in abundance. I have learnt it is common for people to lie in the workplace, and I have witnessed some of the most aggressive and exaggerated lies at work, often to the extreme detriment of others. Such people are Baggers.

Rather than becoming too focused on both ends of the continuum, malicious lies and little white lies, I wish to focus on the majority: Those Blaggers that answer questions without knowledge, make statements that are factually incorrect. Some Blaggers will make decisions in the absence of information, knowledge or experience, and such a character is closely related to the 'Astronomer' character (see Chapter 10). Raising hopes and gaining trust by lying is a trait of this character. People who claim a full knowledge and understanding of something whilst making an effort to cover-up their lies or incompetence are Blaggers.

These people offer opinions, sometimes strong opinions, on topics they claim to have knowledge and experience in. They confidently deliver information, regardless of whether it is factually correct or not. They take every opportunity to sell their ability to their peers, despite a huge amount of personal insecurity and lack of talent. What is more concerning is that others listen and take action as a result of their advice. A Blagger in a senior role within a company is thus a disturbing prospect.

It is very common for insecurity to be the core reason why people evolve Blagger tendencies, especially with regards to the workplace. I have seen Blaggers born in work environments, in order to secure respect from peers and to be taken more seriously in the workplace.

Real Example:

A Project Manager simply lacked knowledge in their role. This is not necessarily a bad thing: I believe people learn and grow into roles, and some roles can and should accommodate a learning curve. However, this person had been in their role for a long time, it was a safety critical role and one where competence was an absolute must: They were responsible for managing a range of sub-contractors. The contractors would often seek clarification on scopes of work or submit technical queries. The technical queries were commonly submitted via email, giving this person the perfect cover to hide under, whilst the Blagger investigated and responded. Their responses to emails would consist of technical information gathered from a variety of trusted sources, largely other people, giving a perception of knowledge and professionalism from the Blagger. Not too much wrong so far…

However, some queries arose in meetings and, rather than this person saying 'I do not know the answer to that question - can I get back to you'? Instead, they would answer the query, regardless of knowledge and consequence. This person would answer confidently and in a convincing manner; they had developed a dangerous talent for blagging in situations.

One technical query, related to the stress of a steel product. The product had to be treated in such a manner that movement of the metal would not take place under particular temperatures. This was a safety critical element of the project. The sub-contractor asked whether the product being provided was stressed and, without any knowledge or hesitation, the Project Manager said "yes", backing his assertions up with other technical 'buzz' words he had picked up over time. He was so convincing, I thought he must know what he was talking about and thought nothing of it. Shortly after the meeting, however, the Project Manager asked a colleague: "What does stress mean?"

Needless to say, this shocked those he told. It was more shocking that he had provided incorrect safety information to a sub-contractor, who would then go on to make other safety critical decisions based on this information, putting people at risk. There had to be intervention and there was.

Once upon a time, a turkey was chatting with a bull. "I would love to be able to get to the top of that tree", sighed the turkey, "but I haven't got the energy". "Well, why don't you nibble on my droppings?" replied the bull. "They're packed with nutrients". The turkey pecked at a lump of dung, and found that it gave him enough strength to reach the lowest branch of the tree. The next day, after eating some more dung, he reached the second branch. Finally, after a fourth night, there he was, proudly perched at the top of the tree. He was soon spotted by a farmer, who shot the turkey out of the tree. Moral of the story: Bullshit might get you to the top, but it won't keep you there.

The Clever Bit:

Children begin lying in order to test boundaries, to get out of trouble or to get what they want. However, their lies are not malicious. People will also lie to protect their feelings, to look good, to gain financially and to avoid punishment. Others lie to avoid being saddled with responsibility (Duckers and Divers). Antisocial personality (ASP) disorder is the diagnosis for people who lie a lot and do so for personal gain. The cause ASP is unknown, but some evidence points to inherited traits and dysfunctional family life.

Sometimes Blaggers are pitied by the person they have deceived. The victim views the liar as deluded and feels sorry for them. It is not unusual for lying to get worse over time, and the cycle is perpetrated as the liar tells more tales to cover themselves.

Workplaces in which there is a high level of competition amongst peers often induce lies. People tend to lie at work as a result of them being discredited and to get even with rival colleagues. People who are habitual procrastinators often lie; for example, many people feign illness or some other 'emergency' to explain away the fact that they've not finished their work on time. Messers and Blaggers are closely linked.

Sometimes, Blaggers lie as a result of delusion; they believe that the truth is not acceptable without sugar-coating it, and that a little embellishing of the facts will not hurt anyone.

A Few Ways to Spot a Blagger:

- They have a selfish outlook and are biased.
- A sense of insecurity is common.
- They lie or bend the truth regularly.
- They tend to be incompetent and lie to protect themselves.
- They will tell you what you want to hear to avoid confrontation.

If you are trying to work out if someone is a Blagger, ask them a technical question they won't know the answer to and see if they try to answer...

If a technical question is not appropriate, ask the following question: How big is Mount Everest? A lot of people know it is big, and many will know it is the tallest mountain on earth. Not many, however, will know how tall it is. Those with Blagger tendencies will give you an answer regardless. Most will say they don't know the answer and hazard a guess, which is also a Blagger tendency. It is a largely irrelevant challenge, in terms of your business, but it tells you a little something. Imagine if these people were to answer critical business questions in this manner. Sadly, people do...this stuff happens. Incidentally, the size of Mount Everest is 8,848 m (29,029 ft)

What Impact Can They Have?

Blaggers may have an extreme impact on achieving goals by creating misdirection through their lies or 'embellishment of the truth'. The bent information provided by a Blagger may be used to make a decision, take action or follow a particular route, and this may result in a dead end or a costly lesson. Lies and confusion are inefficient.

The cost is not only wasted time and other resources used in travelling in the wrong direction, but also to the cost of missing other opportunities. There are also costs associated with correcting a decision or action that was built on a lie.

Once bitten, twice shy! Once someone has been found out that they have been misguided, due to lies, trust is lost. This will make more conscientious managers or colleagues sceptical of the information provided, especially by a proven Blagger. Extra effort and resources will be applied, in order to check that information is trustworthy, slowing decisions and wasting precious time and opportunities. This will harvest 'quality control' actions, which are less efficient than 'quality assurance'.

If a Blagger exists in a team, would people delegate work to them? Probably not or at least rather reluctantly! Instead, the work may be delegated to someone less competent or may be done by yourself, in order to ensure success. Again, this diverts time and resources from other tasks people should be doing. Blaggers do less work, while their reward stays the same. This is a vicious circle.

Philosophical Conclusions.

I'm not upset that you lied to me. I'm upset that, from now on, I can't believe you - Friedrich Nietzsche.

Chapter 3: Flappers

Who Are They?

A Flapper is a character who is not very good at reacting to challenges and crumbles under pressure. They struggle to handle problems in a calm and collected way, and tend to be illogical and panicked when working through an issue.

A Flapper is a delicate character, especially as pressure is subjective. Stress is caused by prolonged, excessive pressure and is a real and serious issue for many people and costs industries millions of pounds a year. All managers need to be tactful and cautious when using pressure to motivate people, as some respond negatively (the 'fight or flight' response is a physiological reaction to a perceived threat). A Flapper is **not** someone suffering from excessive pressure or stress: Furthermore, actions that are intrinsically linked with intense pressure, such as making tens or hundreds of colleagues redundant or undertaking critical life decisions is not part of this equation.

I am referring to the range of situations in the middle of the two extremes that should be fundamental to a role: Those people who crumble when reacting to a delivery challenge, or are flustered when confronting an employee regarding an issue or addressing a customer complaint.

Flappers tend to make every effort to avoid a task or challenge at all costs. Flappers procrastinate and flap about like a panicked bird, thus not getting the job done. They exaggerate situations unnecessarily, claiming that the challenges they face are too big and use extreme language.

This may seem like a grossly insensitive chapter, but it isn't. Companies require strong and balanced leaders who can handle particular situations well and manage them to the best outcome.

Flappers may crumble in silence, but, more commonly, these people are unable to hold it together and demonstrate panic in a physical and verbal sense. They may react irrationally, making poor decisions and negatively influencing others. They are similar to water, in following the path of least resistance.

Have you ever experienced a peer or a manager make such a fuss in a particular scenario, or in terms of a decision based on bad news or a problem that requires a rational view in order to develop a solution? Have you ever experienced verbal or physical outbursts in relation to a concern, which appears to be both inappropriate and inconsistent with the issue? These people are Flappers.

Real Example:

There was a manager who was difficult to get hold of and a tornado of a man. His management style was aggressive, leaving a trail of devastation behind him. He whipped up a frenzy before moving on, leaving the department heads to pick up the pieces and make sense of what had occurred, salvaging anything they could.

Unfortunately, he involved himself in conversations that took place between department managers. The department managers were calmly discussing what options they had, in combatting a particular challenge. The challenge was that several key members of staff had resigned; they had a skill-set and experience that was hard to replace. The manager in question reacted in a flap. He quickly bulldozed his way into the conversation, making rash suggestions such as 'pay them double' and 'close down this department if we can't find anyone'.

After he had calmed and had the options explained, he allowed the department heads to implement their plans as they had wanted. Needless to say, the problem was resolved and with much less fuss.

Sadly, his meddling and flapping at the start put wheels in motion that damaged the company: Many workers heard him over-reacting, which caused panic amongst the workforce. The department managers had to work hard for weeks afterwards in regaining the trust of the workforce, explaining the department would not be shutting down.

The Clever Bit:

Some people will have had bad experiences, in that some situations can create a very real picture of what might go wrong in the future. This perceived picture/outcome can be too big for people to see past and thus may impede the ability to see alternative options.

Flappers simply do not respond to testing times well, and fail under pressure. How do golfers miss a critical putt from 12 inches, when they achieve this all day, every day in training? It's tempting to dismiss such failures as 'just nerves', but, according to University of Chicago psychologist Sian Beilock reports that such outcomes are preventable and a result of information logjams in the brain. Mere laziness cannot explain away the fact that many otherwise well-prepared people do not perform well under pressure.

Anxiety and self-doubt play important roles in this phenomenon, while other researchers think that there is something more fundamental going on. Research into what is known as 'working memory' has proven influential in understanding why some people perform poorly under pressure.

Working memory refers to the short-term memory that we use to solve problems. It's known that anxiety or other unpleasant emotions can reduce available working memory, and this knowledge can lead to a prediction about the impact of working memory during a highly-pressurised testing situation. Perhaps people who have larger working memory capacity perform better in stressful testing situations? After all, if everyone's working memory is reduced by anxiety, then the people with larger working memories will still be better off.

A Few Ways to Spot a Flapper:

- They make random and irrational suggestions/excuses.
- They immediately jump to the worst-case scenario.
- Perspective is lost.
- They are lacking in logical plans.
- They are rarely calm and calculated, when facing adversity.

What Impact Can They Have?

Flappers create an uncomfortable situation and an atmosphere that is not conducive to a positive working environment and sound decision-making. This distorts the view of colleagues and damages work done previously. For example, what if the company reiterates that safety is paramount and should not be compromised at any cost, but a situation arises in that a product needs to be packed and issued to a client immediately, in order to make the night delivery? If the manager starts to flap to such an extent that the profile of the task is placed above safety and should be delivered at all costs, taking short-cuts, this sends out the wrong message, reinforces unsafe behaviours and imports risk. This is unacceptable!

Flappers create a false sense of pandemonium and chaos, and a business without order is destined to fail. It is common for Flappers to act like bullies in the workplace; they like to shout and stamp their feet, just like a two-year-old throwing a tantrum. The morale of the workforce is depleted, and additional resources tend to be employed or thrown at the problem. Root causes of problems are never investigated, in order to prevent them from happening again, and thus the same problems will arise in the future. People may achieve their goals with a Flapper, but it will be expensive!

Philosophical Conclusion:

Fear cannot be banished, but it can be calm and without panic; it can be mitigated by reason and evaluation - Vannevar Bush.

Chapter 4: Duckers and Divers

Who Are They?

Duckers and Divers have an ability to side-step responsibility. Giving an action to a Ducker and Diver is a bit like nailing jelly to a wall: Nothing sticks! It is common for this character to spend time and effort trying to avoid actions and accountability: They use excuses, diversion tactics and confuse matters to avoid ownership. Some Duckers and Divers may accept responsibility for easy-to-complete tasks, yet dismiss accountability for any incompetence on their part. They are quick to propose others for actions and rationalise their nomination even quicker. People may have found themselves assigned responsibility for something without stepping forward, which can happen when Duckers and Divers step backwards, leaving the person seemingly in the forefront.

If Duckers and Divers do accept responsibility for doing something, this does not necessarily mean they are going to do it. This character dumps their responsibilities on others, under the disguise of 'delegation'. Thus, it can be a concern when a Ducker and Diver is assigned a management role.

Some people (including myself) act as 'rescuers' and are sometimes too willing to help others and take responsibility for tasks in the spirit of progress: This is not always the right thing to do.

Duckers and Divers slow down progress and when in a situation where team members are needed to step forward, take ownership and address things for the greater good, these are the people should not feature in a team. They have selfish traits and are not leaders.

Duckers and Divers also becomes a challenge when trying to get to the bottom of an issue. Despite best efforts, sometimes things go wrong and it is important to understand the extent of the problem and identify the causes. Without knowing the root causes of an issue, it is impossible to fix things, thus preventing a reoccurrence. During an investigation, it will be difficult to get to the bottom of things if a Ducker and Diver needs to be questioned, and this is a problem for proactive and pragmatic managers: They may end up fixing the wrong problem, which is a waste. (I refer to this situation as 'picking peanuts out of poo'. Distasteful I know, but it helps to get my point across)!

Real Example:

A senior manager was tasked to handle a very large and lucrative project their company had just won. It was important that someone take full ownership of the project, but, unfortunately, the person deemed accountable for the project was a Ducker and Diver: He would offload all his work and responsibilities. I would like to use the word 'delegated', but this is not the case. Regardless of the task and the person he gave the task to, his grip on it was the same – light. He would rarely check on the progress of an actions that he had dumped on his team!

The senior manager had to undertake some purchasing in his role, and made it very clear that he did not like to do this. He sought to farm out the purchasing of materials to other people, who had their own challenges and responsibilities to manage. Most people helped, as they perhaps felt that he needed support. Despite his colleagues' wilfulness, they made mistakes, negotiate poor rates or payment terms, as they were too busy or ill-qualified to undertake the task properly. The manager soon had nowhere to turn and would postpone his purchasing duties until the last minute (he was also a Messer incidentally), before booking annual leave and then emailing a list of tasks to be undertaken to others, hoping they would be concluded in his absence. Needless to say, the project he was in charge of suffered, due to the fact that this man ducked and dived out of his responsibilities.

The Clever Bit:

Some people fear accountability and failure. They tend to be pessimistic about outcomes and expect failure, and to own a task would thus be admitting failure: Overcoming this fear is a key attribute of good leaders. Avoiding responsibility is a socio-psychological marvel whereby a person is unlikely to take responsibility of an action when others are present. The individual assumes that others are responsible for taking action or have already done so, and this spectacle rarely occurs when the person is alone.

It is common for people to think that avoiding responsibility is lazy. Indeed, responsibility is sometimes avoided due to a lack of motivation, and is not necessarily due to a lack of mobility. Various factors that lessen motivation are a lack of self-efficacy, lack of emotional support, lack of recognition, lack of self-discipline, lack of interest in the task itself, ambivalence, fear of failure and a pessimistic attitude.

A Few Ways to Spot a Ducker and Diver:

- They do not volunteer for work.
- They do not wilfully offer support.
- They tend not to proactively seek clarification.
- They tend to be selfish.
- They make excuses, in terms of accountability.

What Impact Can They Have?

A Ducker and Diver can have a considerable impact on a business. They will slow down progress, creating smokescreens and diversions. They do not to take responsibility, close actions or contribute in a positive way. These characters create frustration in teams, where colleagues wish to progress, impress, improve and achieve targets. Duckers and Divers, simply do not deliver on their actions and missed deadlines cost time and money, and can damage a company's reputation.

Duckers and Divers may over-simplify a topic resulting in poor planning or appreciation of risk. Problems then arise in the project and time is wasted in reacting to them. Some leaders who are Duckers and Divers may pay little attention to detail and thus prevents sound direction and decisiveness, causing further delays. Things get missed and drop through the cracks.

A Ducker and Diver may also work from the opposite end of the continuum, whereby they exaggerate a situation, in order to ensure that an issue is escalated and not owned by them. This causes considerable down-time, and requires expensive meetings and decisions to address the exaggerated problem.

Philosophical Conclusion:

It is easy to dodge our responsibilities, but we cannot dodge the consequence of dodging our responsibilities - Josiah Charles Stamp

Chapter 5: Reactors

Who Are They?

An Reactor is a character that simply responds to situations, rather than being proactive. Reactors often refrain from investing time and effort in planning, commonly believing it to be a waste of time. Despite great planning, things can, and sometimes do, go wrong: This is why it is essential to identify hazards, manage risk and have contingency plans in place. Planning is essential! It is important that, when things do go wrong, those in charge react calmly, quickly and effectively, unlike a Flapper in Chapter 3. Reactors can find themselves in a rancorous cycle. Reactors tend to be unable to visualise or relate to the end game and focuses purely on the now.

A Reactor spends a lot of time trying to put things right that they have not foreseen or planned for. *Fail to plan, plan to fail.* This character often claims they have bad luck, blaming failure on various circumstances and using excuses when things go wrong. A Reactor is similar to the Victim character in Chapter 7 and rationalise.

Reactors rarely contribute to continuous improvement or preventative actions, their horizons are near and spend very little time future gazing. Instead, they only take action following a failure or when they are prompted by someone like a manager. Those people who regularly leave actions from meetings until the last minute to complete them are Reactors. They tend to think only about the here and now, are generally optimistic and are poor at strategising.

A wise person once said that one of the most productive things they did in their working week was to spend one hour thinking. Reactors, will find excuses not to think, like that they are too busy.

Being proactive, showing initiative and aiming to foresee challenges is very important in business and in our personal lives. Risk assessment and business continuity plans are examples of preventative actions and planning. This is proactive management! Being proactive is not just related to relatively sober risk exercises, but can be very effective in doing simple things like making a phone call to check the supplier is still going to deliver the materials ordered on time. If there is a feeling that something is going to go wrong, try and prevent it. *I have found that simply listening to your instinct can go a long way to preventing problems.*

It is widely recognised that prevention is better and, in most instances, cheaper than cure; investing in planning resources often pays dividends. Some Reactors have the skills and experience to foresee potential issues, but, sadly, this rarely translates into action. This character is very good at giving advice and opinions on matters once they have gone wrong. They are the masters of hind-sight: After all, they have ample experience in this. A bad combination is when a Reactor is also a Flapper. Bedlam!

Ask a Reactor what their plan is for the week. Most Reactors will have a list of things they need to do for the day, but few will allocate time and plan when the tasks will be complete. Their plans do not usually consider the resources needed to deliver the plan or what could go wrong with it. Most of the actions on a Reactor's list will be a response to something that has happened or is going wrong.

Real Example:

There was a Purchasing Manager that was responsible for buying and receipting components for a range of products. He had to ensure the components were delivered on time to allow lean manufacturing. His role demanded a huge amount of foresight and, proactivity, in ensuring that the manufacturing and purchasing plan created could be delivered in full.

The Purchasing Manager was very technical, and his experience and knowledge on technical matters was impressive. He would often be called upon to resolve issues with suppliers and purchases made. He found himself forever reacting to issues, mopping up after incidents and never actually fixing anything. He would rarely monitor performance and risk or investigate obvious causes for concern, such as late supply of materials. He would also fail to adhere to the stringent plans and would chop and change them in a reaction to challenges that he should have foreseen. Needless to say, very little was made on time and manufacturing failed to be lean.

The Clever Bit:

Having and meeting deadlines and targets is an important part of our lives. This may bring a lot of pressure, especially within the workplace. Anxiety and fear of failure are often the reasons why people avoid tasks. Appearing stupid and having their sense of self challenged is the greatest concern.

Research has shown that having specific goals and plans help people to focus and thus achieve more. If the proposed plan appears too difficult or the goal is far away, then it can be off-putting to create such a plan; therefore, this action is avoided, which may decrease commitment to the end goal. Those that are embroiled in the detail and have a sense of 'just surviving' are less likely to plan.

Plans are not avoided due to an inability to plan, but are rather the mind-set of 'what's the point', claiming 'it will change anyway!' Another excuse is not having enough time to all the things that need doing. Many of these excuses are due to anxiety or lack of confidence (fear of getting it wrong).

A Few Ways to Spot a Reactor:

- They tend to have no or poor plans.
- A Reactor rarely or incorrectly prioritises actions.
- They would be optimistic and hope things will not go wrong.
- Often, they do not know how to be proactive.
- They tend to have a very close horizon.

What Impact Do They Have?

Sometimes, things go wrong, despite best efforts and it is important to react swiftly, in order to limit any damage and prevent it from happening again. Thus, being adept at being reactive is important, but the volume of reactiveness should be the exception and not the norm.

Reacting to an incident is costly. Some of the costs will be readily visible, such as the cost of fixing the damage caused. Other costs will be less visible, such as the cost of resources to perform an investigations, loss of efficiency and increased insurance premiums, to name but a few.

It would be far less expensive to prevent such incidents from happening. When things go wrong, people become demotivated; they may feel like things do not go right and that they are just 'treading water'. This sense of 'just surviving' makes people feel they are not achieving anything and so they become less productive. The time spent reacting to something that could have possibly been prevented could be spent doing something more proactive, such as getting invoicing done or making that sales call.

Philosophical Conclusion:

Rational behaviour requires theory. Reactive behaviour requires only reflex action - W. Edwards Deming

Chapter 6: Magpies

Who Are They?

Magpies are birds that we loves to hate, and I am not referring to the football team Newcastle United. In many people's eyes, Magpies are the avian equivalents of the football hooligan. In European folklore, the magpie is associated with a number of superstitions surrounding its reputation as an omen of ill fortune. This reputation may derive from the bird's well-known tendency to 'steal' shiny objects.

It is for this reason that I have termed this particular character 'Magpie'. The character is attracted to shiny things, in the form of good ideas, opinions, suggestions, etc and steal them. They trade other people's shiny, polished words and ideas as their own. The Magpie character has a limited imagination, are uninspired and flat. The character is also easily influenced or convinced: They are rarely consistent in their views, which may change quickly, in accordance with the next idea or argument that they hear.

Magpies try to impress their peers by labouring a point they have stolen from somewhere else safe in the knowledge the view is well founded. Magpies will commonly use information in a discussion without fully understanding the concept, source and integrity of the information. Their knowledge of the subject matter is often poor, which can be dangerous if a Magpie is in a decision-making role or is a key influencer.

Leaders or people in management roles that are required to set a strategy, policy or direction are sometimes required to think differently; often known as thinking 'outside the box'. They need to inspire and motivate colleagues, they tend to benchmark, set standards and use best practise, in order to improve. They certainly should not lie, cheat and steal. If found out, this will have the opposite to the desired effect.

I wish to labour the point that it is acceptable to use other people's research, ideas or guidance. I have done so in this book, but it should be made clear if a concept belongs to someone else, and the source of the information should be identified.

I can recall a colleague saying: "I read a lot of books because I am lazy". This confused me, as reading books can be time consuming, and I would not refer to an avid reader as lazy. I asked my colleague to elaborate, and he said: "I read books to learn from other people's mistakes and experiences. This prevents me from having to work it out myself and make costly mistakes". It is this view in part that inspired me to write this book. I hope the book is perceived in a similar way, and may go on to help someone avoid a costly mistake or remedy an ongoing challenge.

Real Example:

I knew someone who worked for a large organisation that employed a large team of administrators, which was managed by a person lacking in knowledge and experience. The manager was viewed in a positive light by the young, inexperienced administrators, and her management style was aggressive and forceful. The direction of the company was weak and they relied on this manager to create policy.

A colleague was reading the company policy on mobile phones, having just received his company mobile. The policy seemed very familiar to him, yet he thought no more of it and continued with his day.

However, in a strange coincidence and set of circumstances, he stumbled across this policy again the following day, but this time it featured the logo of another company. The policy was a word-for-word copy of the other company's policy; worse still, the managing director had signed it. He explained to his colleague that the policy needed reviewing and amending to represent the true values of the company. The incident was embarrassing for many.

The Clever Bit:

I do not want to focus on the act of stealing: I think it's important to consider the drive behind presenting information or actions as your own when they are not. Why do people do this? What is their motive?

Actions are undertaken by people in order to fulfil a psychological need or goal, and masquerading ideas as one's own is no different, apart from it being morally repugnant.

A common reason for such actions is to show off in front of others, and using other people's ideas satisfies this psychological need. Sometimes, the ideas or masked actions are not required by the Magpie, but rather taken from those who are a threat in the workplace, in order to balance things or restore fairness. Jealousy is a powerful factor, in terms of the Magpie character.

Some people will seek attention within the workplace as a result of feeling neglected. A sense of inadequacy or the lacking of knowledge, experience and skills in their role contributes to a motive, with the seeking of compensation as a result. These are possible reasons why people assume a Magpie character.

A Few Ways to Spot a Magpie:

- They have few ideas of their own and lack originality.
- They may be indecisive and quick to 'jump on the bandwagon'
- They rarely go against the grain.

What Impact Do They Have?

Presenting information or ideas that do not belong to you and without a full understanding of the concept can lead to legal action, fines and damaged reputation for all. It can also be a very embarrassing situation. Without a clear understanding of the concept and the integrity of the source, plans may be built on rocky foundations, making them unstable, and this can result in company divestment, having a negative effect on the integrity of management and a drastic drain on resources, in remedying any poor decisions.

Magpie characters tend to be masked within a company: Hidden criminals that compromise integrity. They occupy a valuable position that could be filled by someone much more genuine. This is wasteful.

Some suggestions may be inappropriate and are only put forward by the insecure Magpie for self-marketing purposes. The attention this will attract can divert resources and wastes time, as wild goose chases are sinful.

Philosophical Conclusions:

Desperation is like stealing from the Mafia: You stand a good chance of attracting the wrong attention - Douglas Horton

Chapter 7: Victims

Who Are They?

A Victim is a character who has a perception that they have a lot of bad luck. They think they are devoid of accountability and feel they are powerless to change anything. The Victim character always feels hard done-by, as if an injustice has been done and think life is really hard and always has been. They feel sorry for themselves, uttering phrases such as: "I never get a break" and "Why does this always happen to me"? They feel that their workload is excessive, frequently use extreme terms like 'impossible' and 'unfair', and spend a lot of time criticising and moaning about others, seeking to pin the blame on someone or claiming nobody helps them. The Victim character is negative, downtrodden and slow in their ascent. If the time they spent moaning and complaining was spent getting on with things, they would get more done and would encounter fewer problems. This character believes that they are not in control of things and thus they cannot really influence any outcome. This sense of no or little control will reinforce their perception that the odds are stacked against them. Life happens to these people!

The Victim character is one of three characters in Karpman's Drama Triangle. The drama triangle is a social model of human interaction – the triangle maps a type of destructive interaction that can occur between people in conflict.

I am not referring to vulnerable groups of people that require support. I am also not referring to those with genuine life and work frustration and concerns, including those who are clinically ill with depression or other mental illness: Victims tend not to proactively seek the causes of their problems or in hindsight, meaning that they will continue to make the same mistakes, in approaching successive tasks with the same attitude.

It is not uncommon for a Victim to be presumptuous and paranoid. If a manager makes a decision that the Victim does not like or agree with, this becomes a metaphorical punch to them. If a manager approaches a Victim about their performance, this will be seen as unfair: A Victim tends to have an exaggerated view of their role within the company and, if they are unable to perform their designated role, then this is the fault of someone or something else. Victims simply like to moan, and are not motivated.

Their negative feelings shape their reality, and thus they rarely view things in an objective manner. The emotions of a high-conflict person fluctuate quickly and are intense. Such people have difficulty empathising with others and have a hard time accepting loss and healing from it. A Victim will often be preoccupied with themselves becoming a target of blame and take aggressive action, by engaging in extreme behaviours and losing control of their emotions. They are constantly in distress.

Real Example:

A female barmaid had a really bitter outlook on life. She had been a barmaid at the same pub for over a decade and was very unpleasant to customers.

Over time, many of the customers learnt a lot about this woman. They expected to have learnt how her life was littered with trials and tribulations. This was not the case. She seemingly liked the notion that the customers thought she was unapproachable and miserable. I think she felt this made her unique and gained her attention?

She was rude, negative and simply unpleasant to be around. She would moan about how busy and noisy the pub was and disliked serving people.

Slowly over time, customer stopped going to the pub until it closed. She was unhappy and disgusted to be made redundant and was bewildered why the pub closed. Her bitter cycle continued, the difference this time, she had a real issue to deal with, which ironically fuelled her Victim traits.

The Clever Bit:

Some people blame everyone and everything else for their problems. They are known as 'high-conflict people', and tend to have maladaptive personality traits. In extreme cases, they may display personality disorders, including narcissism. They may possess some self-awareness and promise to change, but this is unlikely.

High-conflict people avoid taking responsibility for their problems, which makes them feel better about themselves. They repeatedly argue against feedback, regardless of how helpful and truthful it might be. Victims try to persuade others to agree with their rigid points of view and to help them attack their targets of blame.

Victims tend to engage in all-or-nothing thinking: They rarely consider different points-of-view, analyse situations or consider possible solutions. They feel like everything is at stake, often feeling like the injured party and thus never learning from their experiences. It is common to hear people saying: 'You would cut off your own nose to spite your face'. This character is guilty of this.

It is common for high-conflict people to try and persuade others to be advocates of their views, and to direct negative attitudes towards the target. This behaviour allows the Victim to avoid confronting their own behaviour and, if this occurs, nothing changes and the high-conflict situation continues. Negative advocates are usually friends, family or colleagues who also blame the target, amplifying the conflict.

A Few Ways to Spot a Victim:

- Victims complain about how bad things are, unnecessarily.
- They tend to exaggerate a situation.
- They believe they have very little influence on matters.
- They take little action in preventing a negative situation.

What Impact Can They Have?

Victims slow progress, wasting a lot of time and resources, in reviewing and addressing their nonsense claims. Discussions with Victims and their perceived view is a real drain, and there is commonly no solution that would satisfy them. It is demotivating.

Victims make biased decisions; they will make rash decisions, often to make a point. This character rubbishes solutions and constructive advice and detracts from other, perhaps more important, tasks. Their mind-set is commonly terminal, and this can be both distracting and contagious to impressionable peers.

Philosophical Conclusions:

A strong, successful man is not the victim of his environment. He creates favourable conditions. His own inherent force and energy compel things to turn out as he desires - Orison Swett Marden

Chapter 8: Non-Believers

Who Are They?

This character is sceptical, cynical and unsupportive of other people's ideas and actions; they rarely use positive or encouraging words. An Non-Believer commonly develops an opinion on a matter, regardless of facts. They are ignorant to other people's views, stubborn and unlikely to change their outlook, even if proven wrong, in order to save face. An Non-Believer likes to predict failure or a negative outcome, and is quick to use the term 'I told you so'!

This character takes pleasure in deliberating about the problems and rubbishing ideas or actions, despite having few or no suggestions themselves. They will always find reasons not to do something, assuming that actions taken to try and change a long-standing problem are futile. Younger and enthusiastic employees are dismissed. An Non-Believer is very risk averse, with a false sense of heightened awareness and authority. Their ideas tend to be general and fluid (non-committal) to avoid an accusation of a bad idea.

This character is closely linked with the 'Know it all' character in the next chapter (Chapter 9). The 'Non-Believer' and 'Know-it-all' characters dwell in hindsight, and their views tend to be arrogant. If they do have their own suggestions or take action, they will protect and champion them aggressively.

This character is useful when trying to appreciate the risks of a situation or idea, but the output must be contained and placed within the correct context. It is common to hear the claim that "there are no bad ideas", and I believe this to be true. I think there is nothing wrong in putting forward an idea, regardless of how developed it may be. Putting an idea into a structured forum or in front of the right group of people can help chisel and shape the concept. Embrace ideas; if this is not done, I believe opportunities will be missed. Non-Believers tend to be a blocker/drain in this process if unmanaged.

Sometimes, Non-Believers can be born within an organisation. They may evolve from no or poor communication, or empty promises. An Non-Believer feeds off procrastination and the grapevine. This character is often bloated by overfeeding on gossip and digests incorrect information. They believe that a conspiracy exists and suspicion is a common emotion, regardless of the facts.

Thomas Edison failed 999 times before he succeeded at inventing the lamp. When he was asked how he managed to continue, in spite of failing all those times, he said: "Whenever it didn't work, I would never say that I failed. I would just say that I had found another incorrect way to make a lamp".

Real Example:

A Manager had spent many years shaping and pruning his team. He had trained them all to a clinical level, or so he would have you believe. He often claimed: "These guys are the best in the country. You won't find anyone better".

Unfortunately, despite his close relationship with his team and heavy personal investment, two of his best team members decided to leave; they had been at the company a long time and decided to take a less stressful, yet more rewarding, opportunity. This came as very bad news to the business, and had a dramatic impact on the Manager. The Manager felt that their desire to leave was the fault of others and that they could not be replaced. He claimed that bringing in agency workers to fill the gap temporarily was not an option and the loss of his team members would be devastating. The manager formed a coup with senior management, and rumours spread about the impending demise of performance like wild fire.

The senior management team decided that, in view of the short notice period, the employees were contractually obligated and, with tight deadlines for work looming, they had no other choice than to secure the services of agency workers. This did not sit well with the Manager, who was acting like an Non-Believer, as he felt that this plan was destined to fail. He complained, procrastinated and was extremely disruptive. Yet he offered no alternative solution, despite extreme efforts to engage, consult and involve him in the process.

Soon, CVs were being reviewed, interviews were taking place and work tests were undertaken. Despite the spiteful manner of the Manager, within three days, two replacement agency workers had been appointed. They were inducted and started work quickly. After a short period learning the job, the agency workers were quicker, better and more hungry than the employees that had left, and were soon outperforming them by 20%. Despite this fact, the Non-Believer refused to acknowledge the progress of the agency workers and made great efforts to discredit them.

I am delighted to say the agency workers went on to be full-time employees of the company, and well respected equals.

The Clever Bit:

In the 1952 Olympics in Helsinki, Roger Bannister set a British record in the 1500 metres, which fuelled his desire to be the first person to run a 4 minute mile.

It was thought that a man could not run a mile in less than 4 minutes, and this belief was unchallenged for many years, until Roger Bannister proved that this was not true. He achieved this feat on 6 May 1954. In the same year, another 37 runners broke the record, followed by hundreds more in successive years.

I wonder if any of the 37 runners had tried hard enough, before Roger Bannister, they could have beaten the record? They simply didn't try, as they thought that trying was futile: This is a similar outlook to the Non-Believer.

People tend to reject ideas for a few reasons, such as conflict in their belief system and knowledge, or more appropriately, lack of it. If people were told something that they always believed to be true, was incorrect, such as the earth is not round, they would tend not to believe it.

Generally, people are not happy taking risks. Nobel prize-winning psychologist Daniel Kahneman once wrote; "for most people, the fear of losing $100 is more intense than the hope of gaining $150. Therefore, some believe that 'losses loom larger than gains' and that people are loss averse." This infers that Non-Believers feel they have something to lose and they do not want to risk it by being positive and supportive about something that may fail. It is easier and safer to be negative.

Some Non-Believers are also perfectionists. Perfectionism can lower confidence, making people sceptical and preventing progress. A task not done perfectly is a task that was not done properly and the task will be repeated over and over again, in order to achieve the perfect outcome. Alternatively, the task is avoided completely, in order to prevent disappointment.

A Few Ways to Spot a Non-believer:

- Their morale can plummet easily and quickly.
- They instigate or thrive off gossip.
- They lack vision and innovation.
- Resistant to change and may purposefully slow progress.
- Have a forceful opinion, but are poorly informed.
- They tend to be very sceptical and cynical.

What Impact Can They Have?

An Non-Believer can have a big impact on morale. Not only do they hamper their own drive and focus; they also negatively affect others. The negativity of Non-Believers is contagious like Measles. It can have a real impact on co-operation, co-ordination and productivity. Productivity decreases, quality of work decreases, mistakes are made, costs increase and profits are lost.

This character captures the attention of others, in wasting time moaning about things they do not believe in. This person and others around them thus become less effective, and time and other resources are wasted as a result. Non-Believer employees do not make suggestions or pose ideas, and their lack of engagement hampers the company by reducing its resilience, preventing it from being dynamic. A rigid and bitter company or employee is very costly and ineffective. Any change suggested or imposed is resisted and extra resources are used, in ensuring a smoother transition, pandering to their lack of engagement. Decisions on everything are slowed, progress throughout the company is slowed, and people become frustrated.

Philosophical Conclusion:

We all have our own life to pursue, our own kind of dream to be weaving, and we all have the power to make wishes come true, as long as we keep believing -.Louisa May Alcott

Chapter 9: Know-it-alls

Who Are They?

A Know-it-all character is a bit like the many 'armchair football managers' throughout the world. These football managers sit in the comfort of their armchair at home, away from the pressure of the game, often with unproven skills and experience, yet seemingly know the solution to their team's poor performance lately or the formula for winning. Their football team never loses, because they never play!

This character shares many similarities with the Blagger in Chapter 2 and the Non-Believer in Chapter 8, as they tend to have an answer for everything. A Know-it-all character act like the world belongs to them and others are in their world. They assign a value to people, where the value is based on helping the Know-it-all to achieve things or making them feel good. It is common for the Know-it-all character to see other people's opinions as less valuable than their own and compassion is seen as a weakness.

Know-it-all characters, as the name suggests, believes they know it all. This character appears to have 'been there and done it' and they know best, regardless of actual skills and experience. They accept very few opinions and ideas from others, and it is a challenge getting them to learn new skills or to change. Know-it-alls often have a false, but heightened, sense of knowledge. They focus on what I call 'the killer statement'. These are statements that are 'eureka moments'. I have seen many discussions lost due to 'killer statement' tennis.

It is common for this character to be over confident, often demonstrating bravado. Challenges from others are met with hostility and aggression and any admission of being wrong is given lip-service and quickly dismissed. They will exaggerate their experience, skills and the value of their contribution, in an effort to self-market and persuade and coerce others into thinking they are knowledgeable. The success and ego of a Know-it-all is highly important to them and will ignore low value tasks. Sometimes, their claim of experience can be a tedious link; a bit like claiming they could fly a plane because they sat in a cockpit once. A Know-it-all will dismiss discussions they are uncomfortable with.

Real Example:

A local football team was managed by a man who seemed very clever and fun to impressionable children. He also appeared as a good leader of boys and a role-model. He was everything a football manager should be.

He gave advice on life as well as football and was an agony uncle to all. He seemed to Know-it-all, which was seen as an admirable to young boys. As the team mates got older and grew from boys to young men, the perception of him started to change.

The team noticed things like how much alcohol he drank and that he was never at home with his family. His Know-it-all trait stopped being admirable and became irritating. He had an answer for everything and his team felt it was hilarious listening to some shambolic answers he gave to questions (the joke was on him). Some of his advice and opinions became a cause for concern with some parents. Many parents had 'off-the-record' discussions with him.

I met him many years later by coincidence where we reminisced. I was very aware that he was still spinning the same yarn, living in the past and much of what he said was irrelevant. I learnt he was jobless, an alcoholic and divorced. I still had an appreciation for him and that he gave up his time to help many boys play football. However, his views and approaches had pushed everyone away, he knew best and was not prepared to concede. It was sad, but despite his shameful situation, he refused help and still felt he was in a position to give advice that he was clearly not best placed to do. He was a Know-it-all.

The Clever Bit:

People want to be noticed and will make efforts to impress people, in order to be noticed. If they are not seen, this makes them feel bad and can cause an unconscious level of arrogance. Arrogance is a sub-conscious defence mechanism: It can make people feel more important, and helps heal a wounded ego. Know-it-alls will act arrogant towards those they feel are less worthy than themselves.

Arrogant people are usually those who fail to be respected by others who are important to them, and they have found no other solution than to gain respect, by force, from those who appear to be less important to them.

People may also have a superiority complex. This type of complex arises when a person who suffers from an inferiority complex decides to act superior, in order to mask their inferiority. The person with a superiority complex usually claims that their opinion is better than others' and more important than their peers. Sometimes, superiority complexes are coupled with self-confidence. Some people have developed a feeling of confidence in a certain field, based on true facts they know about themselves. This just means that they know themselves well and are confident in this.

A Few Ways to Spot a Know-it-all:

- They have an answer for every question.
- Dismisses or treats all ideas and suggestions as pedestrian.
- Thinks no more of their mistakes, blaming others instead.
- Reacts badly to people challenging their views.
- Needs to be wanted or liked.
- Demonstrates arrogance.
- Has a disproportionate sense of self-confidence.

What Impact Can They Have?

In a work context, a Know-it-all can be very dangerous, they may override procedures, instructions and guidance, as a result of them thinking they know best. They can compromise safety, quality and profit, as a result of their ignorance.

Time may be wasted discussing an issue at length, which tends to be the result of a Know-it-all not accepting a change or another person's opinion. Resulting discussions may conclude in arguments and political games, due to a Know-it-all wanting to protect their honour: This may cause frustration, aggression and demotivation amongst colleagues. It can prevent suggestions and ideas being proposed and thus solutions to problems are not discussed and agreed. If a Know-it-all character is in a management position, this can lead to a dependent workforce and loss of initiative. Know-it-all managers may demoralise others, be rude, derogatory and hamper continuous improvement. A company or department will only ever be as good as a Know-it-all manager. Others learn from the bad habits of a Know-it-all, especially young and impressionable employees. It is not uncommon for strong Know-it-all characters to have an army of followers.

Philosophical Conclusion:

The only true wisdom is in knowing you know nothing - Socrates.

Chapter 10: Astronomers

Who Are They?

An actual Astronomer does their job from far away from their subject matter. They work from a distance in a safe and cost-effective place than their counterpart; an Astronaut. There is an obvious reason for this set-up, but for the benefit of my metaphor, Astronauts go, see, touch, feel and do, where Astronomers, like the character do their bit from afar, sometimes locked behind a desk or in an 'Ivory tower'. This is how the name of the Astronomer character originated.

The Astronomer character commonly holds a management or supervisory role. This character makes unsighted decisions and gives direction. Decisions tend to be made without consultation with those who do the job and may be better placed to make a more informed decision. Many of the decisions tend to be inconsiderate or inadequate. Making isolated decisions from the comfort of the boardroom without front line facts is naïve. It's a bit like betting a big stake on the winner of the Grand National horse race based on the name of the horse or colour of the jockey's jersey. Something my family and I do for fun each year at the cost of a quid. This is not a good model for business decision making.

How damaging would a blind decision or prediction be to the morale of the workforce and the integrity of a decision maker if it was wrong, particularly if it was avoidable and unforced?

The Astronomer tends to go with a hunch, in making decisions. This character has similar traits and tendencies as the Box Ticker character in the next chapter (Chapter 11) and make claims to justify their action: They consider this term a plausible excuse when things go wrong. This character may claim it is better to make a wrong decision, than not to make a decision at all. They may make decisions in areas of expertise they have no knowledge of and are often unaware of the potential consequences of their decisions, like the Know-it-all character in Chapter 9.

It is widely accepted that everyone cannot be satisfied in making decisions, but decisions must be based on as much information as possible. It is understood that leadership and some decisions need to be made with limited information. (I am not referring to this scenario). I am referring to those people who continuously make blind decisions and observations, despite access to the right information or data. This is lazy and unprofessional. In many cases, the Astronomer character acts braver from behind the best and out of site.

Real Example:

It is not unusual for industry to be governed by standards and legislations that are enforced and audited by an external body or enforcing agency. This is common in the rail, car and aerospace industries. I have been fortunate enough to have worked in such industries, and have thus experienced the high level of technical expertise required to ensure compliance and safety.

Some standards and legislations demand a particular level of competence, or a particular role must exist within the organisation, such as a 'competent person'.

A Managing Director was reviewing the costs incurred by his company, as he usually did on a monthly basis, and he noticed that a lot of costs were attributed to ensure compliance within a particular industry his organisation was working in.

Unfortunately, by just reviewing the numbers and not understanding them in full, he decided to cut costs by making a few members of the team redundant. This decision was based on a ratio of sales staff vs support staff he liked to employ. Needless to say, his decision was unsighted and had consequences.

The Managing Director learned that he had exposed the business to excessive risk, and that this had compromised the business he was trying to protect. Some of the risks controlled by the people he made redundant were realised; this did not only damage the reputation of the business, costing them a client and legal proceedings. An expensive consultant on very high day rates, costing the company much more than the Managing Director had hoped to save in the first place had to be engaged. This was a catastrophic blind decision made by an Astronomer. (I am sure some of you may be thinking this is unique and does not take place all of the time, but you would be surprised).

The Clever Bit:

One of the reasons why people may act like an Astronomer is because they simply lack good personal skills. Such managers, who lack emotional intelligence, tend to practice avoidance and hide away. They do not like confrontation and have an undeveloped ability to address uncomfortable situations. The usual response to this is to turn-off, just like the Ostrich character in Chapter 13, or, more commonly, to blame others for their failings. This provides a cover or an excuse as to why a decision was made. They claim that the decision is a forced one, so that they can abstain from the consequences. This approach is learned and can be a habit from childhood, previous work situations, or even both.

Some Astronomer characters may be passive-aggressive. They express themselves indirectly, and often in a hostile manner: This may take the form of sarcasm or stubbornness. Research indicates that most employees prefer to be told the truth and to be honestly informed of their failings. A 'back-stabbing' manager, who performs political manoeuvres, commonly demonstrates passive aggressive behaviours.

A Few Ways to Spot an Astronomer:

- They make blind decisions.
- Working in isolation and can be frivolous with information.
- They are rarely seen where and when it counts.
- Tricky communication is via others or when out of site.

What Impact Do They Have?

Decisions made by an Astronomer are dangerous and will have a huge impact on the morale of the workforce: They will create divides and revolutions. Such visionless decisions will also contribute to gaps in processes and create blind spots, if they are not well thought out.

Those responsible for delivering these decisions will have to live with the consequences, which are far from ideal and are sometimes costly. Some Astronomer decisions are based on motives that may have a real impact on other objectives, or the possibility of achieving goals.

The cost of blind decisions is difficult to calculate, but such decisions can certainly ruin an organisation, question integrity and create a nervousness in the workforce due to a lack of trust. This is especially true in departments where specialists are employed. Decisions that have an impact upon areas where experts operate will undoubtedly cause havoc.

Philosophical Conclusions:

It is hard to imagine a more stupid or more dangerous way of making decisions than by putting those decisions in the hands of people who pay no price for being wrong - Thomas Sowell

Chapter 11: Box Tickers

Who Are They?

This character is not always committed to getting the job done well, and is more focused on getting the job done. A Box Ticker is not attentive to the importance of a job, or the consequence of getting it wrong. Their efforts are more of a gesture and representation of completed work: Quantity over quality. A Box Ticker is rarely engaged and not easily motivated.

Incidentally, I believe in the value of checklists and actually ticking off the task once it is completed in full and to the right standard. They can be very powerful and important. They are a great way to help with routine and ensure actions are not missed. Checklists are used by pilots in preparation for take-off. However, they need to be appropriate. There are disadvantages to checklists too…some people think the use of a checklist can dumb things down and remove flair, the art of a craft and spirit.

(If you are unfamiliar with the term 'box ticking', let me explain: This is like having a list of things to do and, as you do them, you tick off the tasks on your list. However, ticking this box does not tell you how well a task has been done, if it has been completed on time and if it has added value). Sometimes, people complete a task without considering the importance of it, simply completing it in order to tick it off their to-do list. This may be because they were not informed or do not understand the importance of the task.

The term 'box ticking exercise' is often used at work. This usually suggests no genuine commitment to the task, and that the implementation is a means to an end. The term is used a lot when excessive red tape exists within an organisation.

People may also be overwhelmed with their workload and want to get things off their list, in order to focus on things that matter to them. Box ticking may also happen because the task is boring.

The focus of the chapter is not the task, but the people who treat and approach most tasks, regardless of its value, in the same way: As a 'box ticking exercise'. There are many people within a company with this attitude, and they are more prevalent in organisations where people are not held accountable for their actions. A box ticker may say: "I have always done it like this and have never had a problem before."

A Box Ticker may become more sinister and dangerous to an organisation if the role they are doing is safety critical and they simply go through the motions. Thus, the work that some Box Tickers undertake may lack substance and integrity and be a risk. A Box Ticker never really achieves or delivers in their work, and most tend to be viewed as busy fools. Rather than undertake a few tasks that add true value, they undertake many that do not. A box ticking mentality can go undetected if the targets or objectives are superficial, and are given lip-service by employees and management.

I have spent a lot of my career auditing businesses, suppliers and management systems, and it is very common to find a broken audit trail or a loose end caused by Box Tickers.

Sometimes, people become Box Tickers as a result of a poor management style. For example, a manager may ask for capacity planning reports to be completed every Wednesday for review, and these are compiled and submitted on time every week. It is later learned, however, that the manager rarely has time to review the reports and never provides feedback. The manager continues to demand that the reports are completed and submitted, yet the integrity of the requirement is lost. The quality of the report thus diminishes, and the task is relegated to a box-ticking exercise.

Real Example:

A very sales focused organisation that employed many different initiatives to encourage more sales and focus their employees. They devised pay incentives and bonus structures that would reward high levels of activity and sales. If employees made 20 sales calls per day, they were likely to attract 6 opportunities to sell, of which 2 might be converted to a sale and an opportunity to invoice. The company naturally focused a lot of attention on ensuring that staff made the 20 sales calls per day.

The target was set, but the standard was not. Soon, people were making a lot of sales calls and there was a real buzz in the office; it was busy and noisy, a vibe was created and the management team were very pleased with the output. Sadly, sales remained flat.

This occurred because the sales people were calling anyone who would answer the phone. Sales calls were considered complete and targets met (i.e. the boxes were ticked) within 2 hours for most sales people. The 'customers' answering the phone were friends, acquaintances, people they spoke with yesterday, people who were not decision makers and people who did not want to buy anything.

However, there were some sales people that wanted to make sales and subsequent commission and did not focus on box ticking. They spent the last hour of the day preparing for the next day's calls: They arranged telephone conferences the next day, and spoke only with decision makers. They would continue to make calls if they felt that the standard of the 20 calls made were inadequate, ensuring that time was spent selling to clients that were researched and could pay. Needless to say, the sales performance of these employees were much higher, and their ratio were outstanding.

The Clever Bit:

Motivation causes us to take action: It gives us a desire to do things, whether grabbing a coat to keep warm or watching a movie for fun. Motivation is the force that instigates and maintains goal-orientated behaviours.

The forces that lie beneath motivation may be biological, social, emotional or cognitive in nature, and there has been a lot of research and theories concerning motivation; for example, the instinct theory motivates people to behave in a certain way because they are evolutionary programmed to do so. Research has proven that we can influence our own levels of motivation, self-control and discipline. Without this, motivation decreases. If we are not motivated to do a task, then the task will not be completed, or will be reluctantly undertaken. Box Tickers are simply not motivated to undertake tasks, and are also unmotivated by the consequences of getting it wrong.

A lack of interest or lack of faith that the action is worth the effort will influence motivation. People may simply have a greater motivation to do something else. If some priorities are in doubt, we may lack clarity as to why some actions are needed.

Some people will work to satisfy bureaucratic administrative requirements, rather than assessing the actual merit of something. Others do so because they feel it is morally right, just to comply with the instructions or rules. People will accept a manager's right to dictate behaviours and actions, and may fear questioning them.

A fear of responsibility may be another reason why a box ticking mentality is developed. Sometimes, people fear leadership and fear failure, and thus hide behind other people's instructions. They then have someone to blame, in the event of failure.

Those who are pessimistic and cynical, much like the Non-Believer character in Chapter 8, are likely to be Box Tickers too. Such a jaded outlook means that people feel that their effort benefits others, rather than themselves.

A Few Ways to Spot a Box Ticker:

- They simply go through the motions (a gesture).
- They do not understand why the task should be completed.
- Often works without consequence or accountability.
- Poorly motivated, with no incentive to do a good job.

What Impact Do They Have?

Box Tickers may compromise the integrity of a team, in their ability to achieve objectives or goals. They may discredit themselves and others by not completing the task to the correct standard.

Employees that do not think about the value of the job, have no perspective on the reason for the task to be done nor are they engaged in the cause creating a real block in company performance. Managers become overwhelmed in making decisions, checking all actions meet expectations (micro-management), coming up with solutions and ideas. This is a drain on management, increases pressure and making them less effective. Tasks are not delegated, trust is lost, employee skills do not develop and performance can plateau. Introducing ideas and challenging the status quo with a Box Ticker can absorb a huge amount of resources. Changes may be short-lived and the culture of box ticking will quickly revert back to type.

The biggest impact of a Box Ticker is the volume of lost opportunities. The Box Ticker is often where the information is, they can make suggestions to improve things, saving time and money.

Philosophical Conclusion:

I think sometimes we rush through countries, ticking off the attractions, but that's missing the point.- Mem Fox

Chapter 12: Cyclops

Who Are They?

This character tends to have very narrow opinions and is stubborn. Their opinions are often biased, and so reasoning with this character is very difficult. Sometimes, their vision can turn into tunnel vision, in that their point of view becomes very restricted and focused.

Having spent many years playing and watching sports, I noticed there were a lot of similarities between the Cyclops character and avid, die-hard sports fans. Some sports fans strongly believe that their team is the best in the world, despite reality proving otherwise. There is a term I like that is synonymous with this point, and is the reason for me calling this character Cyclops: The term is 'one eye' supporters. I know many sports fans are said to have 'one eye', meaning they only see one perspective. However, this character is found in businesses too.

A view or opinion that is stubbornly maintained and protected, despite being challenged and proven unhealthy, with facts, is detrimental to any business, and is true of the Cyclops character. This character will rarely change their views, even if they are proven wrong. They accept change reluctantly.

Everyone will have an opinion or a belief, most of which will have been shaped subconsciously over time and from different experiences. This is often what makes conversations interesting, and what makes people so diverse and unique. Many organisations have a diversity and inclusion policy that encourages the employment of people from different backgrounds, allowing the company to benefit from a wide variety of views, cultures, experiences and skills. Cyclops characters lose the opportunity to benefit from other people's experiences and views, due to their tunnel vision or single eye approach. A Cyclops is often ignorant or dismissive of other people's views: They tend to believe that someone else's opinion that is different or challenges theirs is wrong or worth less.

Reasoning with or persuading a Cyclops is very difficult. They often hold a grudge, and will rarely let go after an apology or conclusion. Grudges further narrow their view, potentially making them spiteful. Cyclops characters are cynical and have a lot in common with the Know-it-all character in Chapter 9.

It is important to have opinions, and people must protect and believe in their views. It is also OK for people to disagree with them. Be careful not to be fooled by someone protecting their views as a Cyclops. Much like with all of these characters, there is a fine line here, and we should remind ourselves that we are referring to people's dominate traits.

Real Example:

A working man's pub, situated in a relatively deprived area, but not far from an exhibition centre. The pub was often filled mid-week with men after a hard days shift on the tools. It was teaming with trades men like electricians, bricklayers and roofers. The pub was full the weekend with children and their parents.

The pub was run by a committee, made up of aging retired men with strict and biased views. The committee were not pleased with the type of people the pub was attracting. The committee decided it wanted to attract customers from the exhibition centre and spent a considerable amount of money building a restaurant on the back of the pub. Before the funds were found and restaurant built, the business plan was challenged and had many flaws from no marketing budget to recruitment challenges.

The views of the committee members were fixed. Their desire to proceed with the plan was unshakable, despite facts presented to them and opinions from experienced, local business people.

The restaurant was built, opened and closed within 12 months! Staff lost jobs, existing customers became disengaged and pushed away. A lot of money was lost. Beer prices went up to repay the loan and the restaurant was turned into an exclusive committee lounge. Funny that!

The Clever Bit:

People may have selective perceptions, limiting their ability to see things clearly. This can prevent them from living in reality; instead, they live their lives with blinkers on. It is hard work living in such a manner and this increases tension, making people irritable and short tempered.

The Cyclops character tends to become preoccupied with detail, rather than looking at the bigger picture; this shrinks their emotional bandwidth and denies any aspect of reality. There are many reasons why individuals may be this way, and some boil down to fear. People may decide to reject other people's views and other opportunities as a result of such fear, as it is easier and more comfortable to keep their blinkers on. This feels safer and less risky.

Removing the blinkers is like seeing in colour for the first time. Tunnel vision is rigid and constraining, while being open is fluid and liberating. People will realise clarity in removing the blinkers, even if the reality is scary. It is important that a person with tunnel vision ascertains what it is they are scared of, before making an effort to achieve clarity.

How to Spot a Cyclops:

- They tend to have narrow and biased views.
- They have stubborn, unshakeable opinions.
- A Cyclops is difficult to engage with and persuade.
- They ignore the facts they do not want to see or hear.

What Impact Do They Have?

This character may force opinions on others and bully people into decisions, resulting in artificial support of views. Others may feel inferior and thus may avoid voicing their opinions or making decisions, resulting in a sub-servient workforce. This indecisiveness can lead to procrastination and paralysis within the management team, and progress is often halted. Some managers respond to those who shout the loudest, and it is a Cyclops who often shouts the loudest. A scenario where the 'squeaky wheel gets the oil' never works well for the masses: It simply encourages people to shout more and those who are not that way inclined are never heard.

The biased and narrow view of this character may lead to little diversity and the ability to make strong decisions based on a wide range of inputs. Some actions may be blind, as the decision may be based on a single person's biased and narrow view. This can lead to costly reactive efforts, in fixing the fall-out from bad decisions.

A lot of time may be wasted in trying to change the opinions of a stubborn Cyclops, which drains resources and increases frustrations. Thus, others may not want to deal with Cyclops characters, which is bad for team cohesion and morale, and is particularly damaging if the Cyclops is client facing. A team is stronger when it is united in having a common purpose and direction.

Some people are very good at communicating and selling their opinion to others, and, if a Cyclops possesses this skill, it can be very hazardous and costly.

Philosophical Conclusion:

Facts are stubborn things, and, whatever may be our wishes, our inclinations or the dictates of our passions, they cannot alter the state of facts and evidence - John Adams

Chapter 13: Ostriches

Who Are They?

Contrary to popular belief, an Ostrich does not bury its head in the sand when it is scared. However, I will lean on this well-known myth to make my point. Someone who puts their head in the sand (not literally) when challenges or even opportunities present themselves can be problematic. Indeed, hiding and putting one's head in the sand does not make a problem go away. Ostrich characters may live to fight another day, but the problem has not been solved and will remain, possibly reappearing as a much larger problem with more devastating consequences.

The Ostrich character often recognises the challenges they face, but chooses not to act and hide from it. They either ignore the issue, hoping it will go away or take a chance that someone else will resolve it. An Ostrich character addresses challenges and takes opportunities, but they tend to be the small and easy jobs first.

Some Ostrich characters avoid investigating an incident as this may result in actions they do not want to do or feel incapable of executing. Any investigations completed tend to be biased, missing the real root cause. The findings and actions will be ones they want and feel comfortable doing. This character shares many similarities with the Reactor character in Chapter 5.

As the saying goes, 'ignorance is bliss'.

I am a firm believer in that you are only as good as the people around you, and if you are surrounded by Ostrich characters, you will quickly find that your team is weak and consequently you underperform.

How many people can you identify that are aware of a problem and yet do nothing about it? Some people may not be in a position to do anything, but they can report it and refrain from accepting problematic issues. Not taking responsibility to act is also an Ostrich Character trait.

I once knew a gentleman who said "I have stopped looking under rocks now, as I always seem to find something".

Real Example:

A company had experienced several years of difficult trading. Despite their best efforts and a tightening of their metaphorical belt, a profit could not be made. As part of the cost-saving measures, an annual pay rise in line with inflation did not occur. Local competitors, however, were winning large contracts and could afford to pay much higher wages. The best employees began to leave the struggling company; morale was low, absenteeism was high, workmanship was questionable and accident rates were rising.

Despite diligent reporting of issues, concerns and suggested solutions to senior management, very little was done. They were ignoring things and were hiding: The Ostrich effect was definitely occurring.

Initiatives could have been put in place, in order to remedy the problems. There were regular discussions of potential solutions at a local level. The Ostrich traits amongst senior management were crippling the organisation, ignoring the reports from the shop floor.

The Ostrich characters controlling the business were aware of the challenges and knew the output they were experiencing was not favourable, yet they shied away from addressing the issues. The management team seemed to have frozen and claimed efforts were superficial and would be ineffective. The Ostrich characters could not hide much more and started to leave the company. They were replaced by promoting people from the shop floor. The new management team lacked experience, but were motivated to resolve the challenges. They did and the business started to turn the performance around.

The Clever Bit:

People can close their minds and hide from what they fear; sadly, in doing so this may prevent their goals from being fulfilled. Anxiety is a common reason why people may act like the Ostrich character resulting in frustration and procrastination. Sometimes, perception of risk may be exaggerated, causing an imaginary threat. This can increase a sense of fear and subsequent further inaction and restriction. There is a sense of never try and never fail. Feeling self-conscious and expecting rejection are negative and fearful thoughts.

A decision to address the issue, just not right now, is procrastination. Waiting for a better time or a time when the mood is right or feeling more confident is an excuse.

How to Spot an Ostrich:

- They ignore or do not address the true cause of a challenge.
- They tend to perform easy, low priority tasks first.
- They follow the path of the least resistance.
- Lack distinct leadership skills at times when it is needed.

What Impact Do They Have?

Ostrich characters sit back and watch as hazards become realised. They may make colleagues and their company look foolish, which may result in conflict and turmoil. It is a true disappointment to realise that the people in the team have the skills and experience to proactively identify hazards, but have failed to take such risks seriously and do anything about them. They thus place a significant strain on resources to compensate for this, causing further resentment, demotivation and a less co-operative workforce.

Many people pull together to fix a problem, in order to prevent it escalating throughout an organisation. Being unable to make and act upon decisions can be catastrophic to an organisation. Sometimes, people are not very self-aware or receptive to a changing environment and being unable to make key strategic decisions can result in vulnerability. This is a trait of the Ostrich character and is crippling.

Alternatively, opportunities are missed due to a lack of awareness of the surrounding circumstance, and this in turn can cost money. Lost opportunity is expensive: Companies in competitive marketplaces need to keep moving, evolving and developing. They are a lot like a shark in that, if they stop moving, they will drown and die.

Missing the root causes of problems can lead to fixing the wrong thing. Also, without knowing the extent of a problem by poor checks and balanced, it will be difficult to gauge the severity of the concern. This also creates vulnerability.

Philosophical Conclusion:

"The mass of men lead lives of quiet desperation. What is called resignation is confirmed desperation" - Henry David Thoreau

Summary

This book sets out to highlight some characters that may be encountered at work and in our personal lives. By now, you should be able to identify the key personality traits of each of the characters. Here is a quick recap:

Chapter 1: Messers. They procrastinate and stall. Mess about and never get anything done.

Chapter 2: Blaggers. They lie and misguide.

Chapter 3: Flappers. They are indecisive and make an unnecessary and disproportionate fuss.

Chapter 4: Duckers and Divers. They dodge responsibility and never own or close actions.

Chapter 5: Reactors. They are not proactive and work in a reactive manner. Always too late in taking preventative action.

Chapter 6: Magpies. They are attracted to and steal other people's ideas, lack integrity and are easily influenced.

Chapter 7: Victims. Always feel hard done-by, moaning that the world is against them.

Chapter 8: Non-believers. They do not believe in others' decisions or actions. They are never supportive and cynical.

Chapter 9: Know-it-alls. They think they know best and are ignorant and pessimistic.

Chapter 10: Astronomers. Make blind decisions or form blind opinions. Are rarely on the front line.

Chapter 11: Box Tickers. Undertake actions with no real understanding of them. Get a job done, but not always to the required standards.

Chapter 12: Cyclops. Stubborn in their views, which are narrow and biased.

Chapter 13: Ostriches. They never confront or address problems; rather, they ignore them, hoping that they will go away.

What does good look like?

If you are able to identify, eliminate or control these characters, you will be able to get more done, quicker and reap the rewards. Decisions may be made and actions taken quicker to cease opportunity (**no Messers**). Employees within your organisation will not lie or answer questions they do not know the answer to, resulting in no wasted time and wild goose chases, saving time and money. Answers will be sought properly and decisions made on fact (**no Blaggers**) improving integrity of the decision makers. The ability to handle challenges in a smooth, calm and professional manner will instil confidence in many and breed a solution mentality (**no Flappers**).

Not only will the business be better armed to deal with challenges, employees will understand what they are accountable and responsible for and accept the situation when they are at fault. Fixing causes and moving on quickly is important for a healthy and sustainable business (**no Duckers & Divers**). The company will become more progressive and spend valuable time and effort foreseeing problems and proactively intervene; after all, 'prevention is better (and cheaper) than cure' (**no Reactors**).

Having people in your team who are innovative, dynamic and inspirational has a brilliant impact on a company, in ensuring organic ideas are forthcoming and the company reacts well to market changes or unforeseen challenges (**no Magpies**). The benefit of this is a resilient, sustainable and forward thinking company meaning improved possibility of future success and survival. A workforce that reacts well and relishes a challenges and not complain unnecessarily will harvest a positive culture and a 'can do attitude' fixing things and saving time and money during difficult situations (**no Victims**).

People need to believe in decisions, provide support to their peers. Optimistic workers can help nurture a happy workplace, reducing staff attrition, keeping talent in the business and saving on recruitment costs (**no Non-Believers**). A management team and employees that work together and consult on issues, share ideas, seek alternative perspectives will improve engagement, raise standards and broaden horizons (**no Know-it-alls**).

Decisions will be made in consultation and in less haste. They will be made using information and data from the front line, meaning decisions will be better and less time and money spent revisiting the decision or fixing it in the future (**no Astronomers**). The sense of engagement from all will pay dividends in the future, especially in times of hardship. Tasks will not be completed for the sake of it, or for ticking them off the 'to-do' list, but to ensure that a good job is done and that any jobs with no or low value are eliminated and suggestions are made (**no Box Tickers**). The benefit of this is improved efficiency and effectiveness.

People within an organisation should acknowledge other people's views, making efforts to understand them. Differences should be considered healthy, in ensuring the right decisions are made and implemented. Biased and dangerous views are banished, and a workforce should have the power, confidence and management system to attack any challenge head-on, at the first sign of a problem (**no Cyclops**). Any problems or challenges that arise should be confronted and addressed accordingly, in order to prevent recurrence and not hidden from (**no Ostriches**). Effective solutions carry huge value in companies.

There are many benefits in correctly handling the 13 characters outlined in this book. There are other characters in the world, but those discussed here are more common and carry larger consequences. They are out there: Find them!

How to handle the characters

It is one thing recognising the characters within this book, but it is another to eliminate or control them within the workplace. Unfortunately, the method of handling such characters can be very expansive, especially as some of the techniques do not always work in every situation. There are some text book methods but managing people and behaviours is not an exact science. Managers will have to constantly review the situation, inventing different ways of motivating and inspiring people, as well as eliminating and controlling risk.

I have outlined some basic suggestions on how to help handle the characters. It is not always possible to eliminate risk, so you may need to control it instead. This comes at a cost, perhaps in the form of management time and support. The more you micro manage the situation, the cost is likely to increase. Ensure that the control measures you put in place are proportionate to the risk. 'Do not use a cannon to kill a fly'!

The ways to handle the characters are suggestions. It is up to you to interpret the suggested actions in a way that will get the best outcome. This can be influenced by your own management style, the type of role the character is in and the level of maturity of the character to name a few.

How to handle a Messer:

- Provide or suggest clear goals, priorities and deadlines. Try to eliminate conflicting objectives and make them responsible.
- Raise awareness of the consequences of procrastination and ensure good planning and focus is maintained. This can be done through incentives, which incidentally do not have to be expensive or cost anything at all.
- Detail expectations and milestones, providing good time management advice. Eliminate excuses.
- Instigate a change of routine and facilitate a systematic framework in helping to address bad habits.
- Find out what they are fearful of and provide support, such as information, instructions and training.

How to handle a Blagger:

- Set expectations/boundaries, and outline the consequences of 'blagging'. Do not accept delusion.
- Encourage and incentivise honesty by creating an open, fair and blame-free working environment.
- Demand supporting information and evidence for claims. Hold collaborative forums to prevent silo discussions.
- Encourage good team cohesion and set goals or agendas with a common focus on collaboration and team-work.
- Find out the motives behind lying or embellishing, such as personal gain or to discredit someone and address them.

How to handle a Flapper:

- Keep them focused on the goal and ensure perspective; perhaps break the challenge down into smaller, bite-size chunks.
- Prevent knee-jerk reactions by providing an easily accessible reporting and support mechanism.
- Ensure a systematic approach to problems is in place, which they are trained in and can follow.
- Prevent the character from handling any issue in isolation.
- Promote a collaborative approach in problem solving.

How to handle a Ducker and Diver:

- Set clear and unambiguous responsibilities and authority
- Make efforts to motivate this character, instilling confidence.
- Prescribe responsibility and milestones, providing good time management advice and deadlines. Eliminate excuses.
- Eliminate assumptions and review progress regularly, ensuring the discipline of the character is good.
- Provide support to the character, such as advice, guidance, emotional support and recognition.
- Breed consideration into this character, in that they are aware of the impact of no action being taken.

How to handle a Reactor:

- Refer to the actions needed to help control a Messer above; as these two characters have similar traits.
- Train the character on a systematic approach to planning and risk.
- Ensure a plan is developed in a timely manner and that the plan has integrity and is reviewed regularly.
- Encourage the character to future gaze and forecast.
- Inspire the character to forecast reasonably foreseeable risks and be proactive in eliminating or control such risks.
- Focus on preventative actions and ways of reporting concerns quickly.

How to handle a Magpie:

- Educate the character on the legalities of plagiarism and stress that copying is immoral, unacceptable and costly.
- Consider moving this character out of innovative, creative roles.
- Ensure this character receives recognition for good things and is reprimanded for negative actions.
- Provide information, instruction, training and supervision, in order to minimise any inadequacies, which may be their motivation to plagiarise.
- Monitor and manage this character, checking sources of information and focusing on credibility.

How to handle a Victim:

- Create a code of conduct for the character, and ensure that it is adhered to.
- Make efforts to reduce potentially conflicting situations and to increase responsibility for actions.
- Surround this character with strong people who are not easily influenced by their negativity, including a leader.
- Keep them focused and rational and ensure perspective, perhaps through regular interfaces.
- Ensure that a systematic approach to problems is followed and provide mentorship.

How to handle a Non-believer:

- Make efforts to secure their interest and engage them in tasks, in trying to get them to be supportive.
- Manage their level of morale and discuss in detail cynical views, demonstrating otherwise with facts.
- Communicate with the character, regarding decisions, and provide them with feedback during consultation.
- Acknowledge risks, agree an approach to these and act proportionately. This character is risk averse.
- Try to find out what it is they think they have to lose. This character acts in protecting something.

How to handle a Know-it-all:

- Ensure that any interaction is on a level playing field. Their opinions are not worth more than others' opinions.
- Provide honest feedback and positive recognition for this character.
- Try to find out what the character is defensive about; arrogance is a defence mechanism.
- Engage them in conversations and discussions, asking them to justify their views.
- Communicate with them and provide them with feedback during consultation.
- Make them responsible, or even accountable, for their views and actions.

How to handle an Astronomer:

- Acknowledge and help this character develop personal skills and handle confrontation.
- Encourage honesty and provide a simple mechanism for securing consultation for decisions.
- Hold this character accountable for all the decisions they make, eliminating all excuses.
- Provide supporting advice to managers/decision makers (encourage consultation on decisions).
- Explain that political manoeuvres and 'back-stabbing' will not be tolerated.

How to handle a Box Ticker:

- Encourage a sense of curiosity and ask them to understand the reasons why they are doing something.
- Make efforts to motivate this character, instilling confidence and securing an interested and engaged person.
- Prescribe responsibility and eliminate assumptions. Review progress regularly and track discipline.
- Provide support to the character, such as advice, guidance, emotional support and recognition.
- Provide information, instruction, training and supervision, in order to fill any knowledge gaps. Question them on this.
- Provide them with a detailed description of the consequence of a job done poorly.

How to handle a Cyclops:

- Keep them focused on the goal and ensure perspective, perhaps through regular interfaces.
- Ensure a systematic approach to a problem is in place, which they are trained in and can follow.
- Acknowledge risk, agreeing on an approach to this and appropriate action. This character is risk averse.
- Prevent the character from handling any issue in isolation. Provide a collaborative approach.
- Acknowledge their views and empathise with them, but communicate clearly that there are disadvantages to these.

How to handle an Ostrich:

- Acknowledge risks, agreeing an approach to these and acting proportionately.
- Make an effort to reduce potentially conflicting situations and increase responsibility.
- Encourage problem-solving forums and other forms of support, and a means of escalating challenges.
- Break problems down into smaller pieces and work through them together. Attribute mutual responsibility.
- Stress the importance of facing problems head-on, and that prevention is better than cure.

Can you take action?

What is stopping you?

Final thought…

Being consistent is a positive trait, but being consistently bad is not…

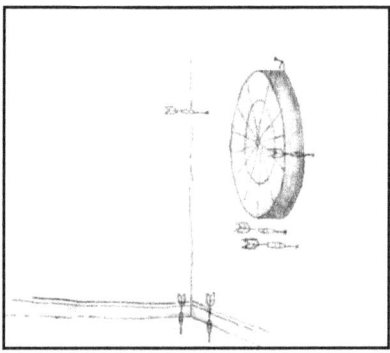

Routine and tradition are not always good reasons to keep doing something…

Bibliography:

http://en.wikipedia.org/wiki/attribution_psychology. Attribution Psychology. (2015)

http://en.wikipedia.org/wiki/self_serving_bias. Self-serving Bias. (2015)

http://www.truthforkids.com/age-characteristics. Age Characteristics of Children. (2015)

http://www.psychologytoday.com/blog/dont-delay. Are Procrastinators Just Lazy? (2010)

http://en.wikipedia.org/wiki/procrastination. Procrastination (2016)

http://www.psychologytoday.com/basics/self-sabotage. Self-sabotage. (2016)

http://www.psychologytoday/blog/compassion_matters. Why we lie and how to stop. (2013)

http://www.buzzle.com/articles/why people lie.html. Psychology behind why people lie. (2015)

http://www.news.uchicargo.edu/article/2010/09/21. Psychology shows why we choke under pressure and how to avoid it. (2010)

http://www.uchicargo.edu/features/20101025_choke. Brain is key to choking under pressure. (2010)

http://www.mostlywind.co.uk/performance_anxiety.html. Mostly Wind. (2016)

http://thecharacterofleadership.co.uk/2009/02/12/fear_and_accountability. Fear and Accountability. (2009)

http://en.wikipedia.org/wiki/diffusion_of_responsibility. Diffusion of Responsibility. (2016)

http://www.psychologytoday.com/blog/evolution_the_self/200806. Laziness: Fact or Fiction? (2008)

http://www.webstandardssherpa.com/reviews/breaking_the_perfectionism_procrastination_infinate_loop. Breaking the perfectionism –procrastination infinite loop. (2014)

http://www.excelatlife.com/articles/self-esteem.html. The Pillars of the Self-concept: Self-esteem and Self-efficacy. (2015)

http://en.wikipedia.org/wiki/goal_setting. Goal Setting. (2016)http://www.psychologytoday.com/blog/dreaming_freud/201408/why_do_people_steal. Why do people steal? (2014)

http://en.wikipedia.org/wiki/attention_seeking. Attention Seeking. (2015)

http://www.psychologytoday.com/blog/stop_walking_on_eggshells/201505. High conflict people. (2012)

http://en.wikipedia.org/wiki/Karpmans_drama_triangle. Karpman Drama Triangle. (2014)

http://en.wikipedia.org/wiki/four_minute_mile. Four Minute Mile. (2013)

http://en.wikipedia.org/wiki/loss_aversion. Loss Aversion. (2015)

http://www.2knowmyself.com/why_some_are_people_arrogant. Why are some people arrogant? (2015)

http://www.2knowmyself.com/superiority_complex. Superiority Complex. (2015)

http://en.wikipedia.org/wiki/emotional_security. Emotional Security. (2015)

http://en.wikipedia.org/wiki/judicial_disqualification. Judicial Disqualification. (2015)

http://en.wikipedia.org/wiki/passive_aggressive_behaviour. Passive Aggressive Behaviour. (2015)

http://en.wikipedia.org/wiki/self_control. Self-Control. (2014)

http://www.verywell.com/theories_of_motivation. Theories of Motivation. (2015)

http://www.psychologytoday.com/blog/emotional_sobriety/201108. When vision becomes tunnel vision. (2011)

www.ingramcontent.com/pod-product-compliance
Lightning Source LLC
Chambersburg PA
CBHW070426180526
45158CB00017B/772